Steve Parish™

KIDS

Nature Learning

BIG
BOOK

of Australian
Backyards

"Help your child uncover the enchanting, hidden world of living things just waiting to be discovered right in your very own backyard."

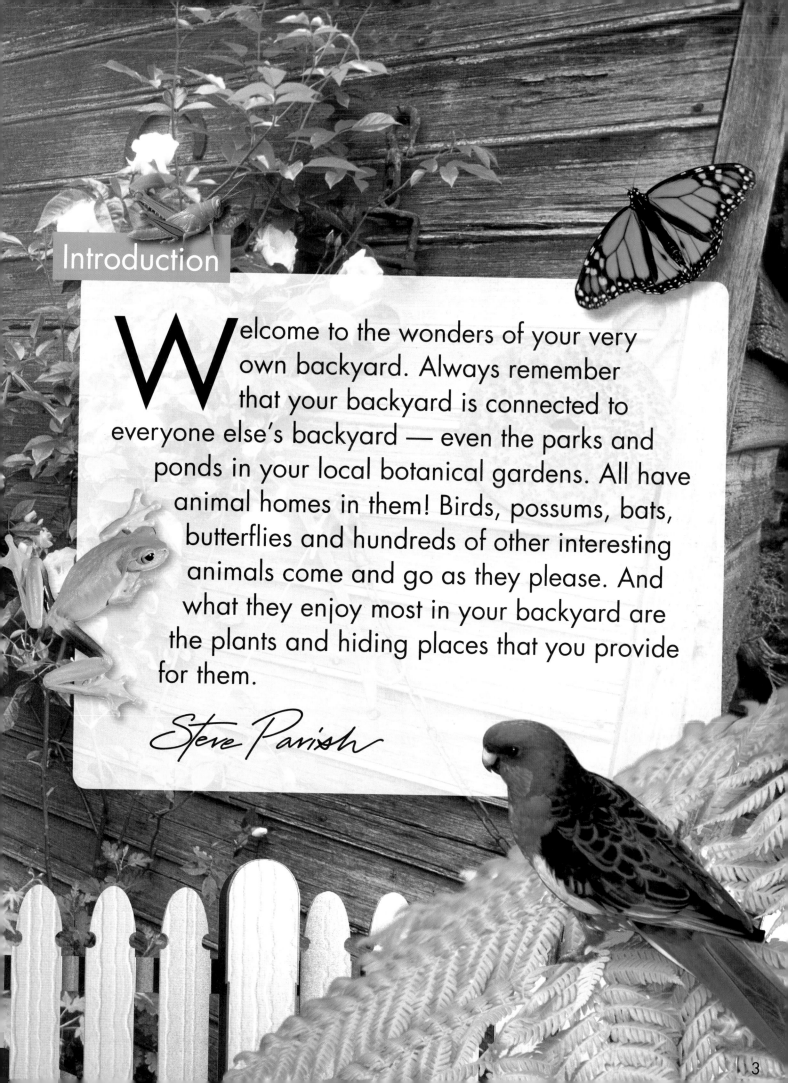

Welcome to the wonders of your very own backyard. Always remember that your backyard is connected to everyone else's backyard — even the parks and ponds in your local botanical gardens. All have animal homes in them! Birds, possums, bats, butterflies and hundreds of other interesting animals come and go as they please. And what they enjoy most in your backyard are the plants and hiding places that you provide for them.

Steve Parish

Welcome to
My
Backyard

Contents

 This icon means that I can scratch, bite or sting.
Don't touch me if you see me in the backyard.

5

What lives in my backyard — covered with fur?

Lots of animals visit my backyard. Some animals wear fur coats; other animals have feathers. Some animals are scaly and other animals... well, you'll have to look at the pictures in this book to find out what the animals are wearing!

Bandicoots

Bandicoots come into my garden at night and often leave holes in the lawn.

Wallabies

Wallabies munch on the lush green grass in my backyard.

Brushtail possums

Possums like to run around on my roof at night.

Ringtail possums

Possums sleep in the daytime and wake up at night.

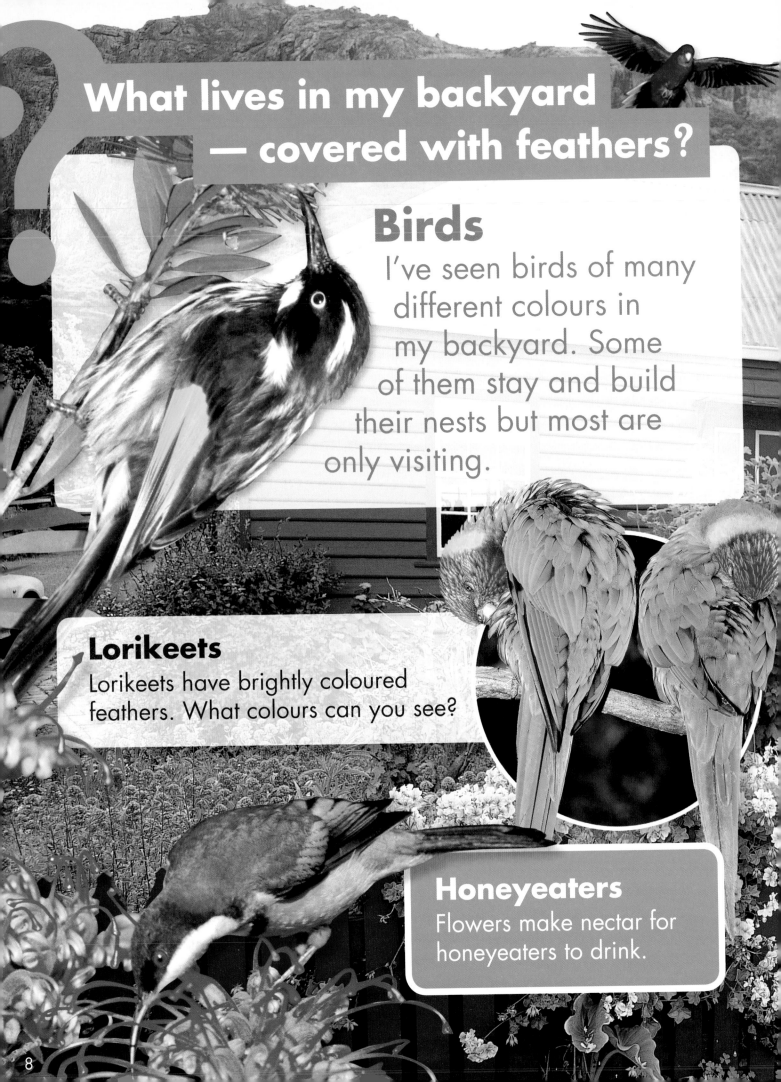

What lives in my backyard — covered with feathers?

Birds

I've seen birds of many different colours in my backyard. Some of them stay and build their nests but most are only visiting.

Lorikeets

Lorikeets have brightly coloured feathers. What colours can you see?

Honeyeaters

Flowers make nectar for honeyeaters to drink.

Rosellas

Red and blue rosellas nibble seeds in my yard. How many rosellas can you see?

Cockatoos

A hole in the tree in my backyard is home to two bright white cockatoos.

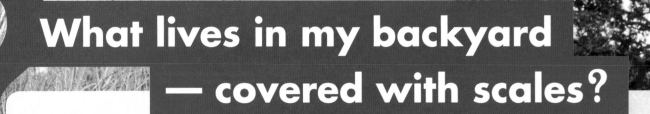

What lives in my backyard — covered with scales?

Snakes & lizards

Snakes and lizards are covered in dry scales. They hide in lots of places in my backyard. Lizards scurry about my garden in the daytime. Some lizards can run very fast on their short stubby legs.

Brown tree snakes

This snake has big eyes and brown stripes. It goes hunting for birds and mice in my garden.

Blind snakes

Blind snakes can't see well. They are very small and live in the dirt and like eating ants and termites.

Carpet snakes

A carpet snake sometimes hides inside the roof of my house.

Blue-tongues

The blue-tongue lizard tastes the air with its brightly coloured tongue, hoping to find a snail to eat.

Bearded dragons

Even though it's called a dragon, this dragon does not breathe fire. Luckily this dragon eats insects — not people!

Garden skinks

Small garden skinks love to warm themselves on rocks or logs in the sun.

11

What lives in my backyard — covered with moist skin?

Frogs
The frogs in my backyard are covered in cold, moist skin. They hide in damp places, close to water.

Croaking
With its loud "*croak, croak*" the bullfrog calls from the gutters after rain.

Tree-frogs
Tiny, brightly coloured tree-frogs are hard to see among the leaves and vines in my garden.

Frog feet
Many climbing frogs have special toes to help them hold onto the leaves in my backyard.

Frog skin patterns

Some frogs are speckled and spotted to help them hide among the shadows in my garden.

Tadpoles

The tadpoles in my pond will lose their tails and grow legs as they change from tadpoles into frogs.

Cane toads

Toads like this shouldn't be in my garden. They eat all the other frogs' food!

13

What lives in my backyard — with 6 legs?

Insects

They creep, crawl, dig and fly through my backyard. Insects have six legs, two antennae, and outside armour.

Butterflies & moths

Some butterflies have taste buds on their feet! They can taste the surface of every leaf they land upon.

Bees

Bees collect nectar from flowers and change it into honey.

Wasps

This wasp is collecting grubs for its babies to eat.

Ants

My backyard is home to thousands of ants. They are tiny but they work together to carry away my lunch!

Beetles

Beetles have hard shiny shells on their backs to protect their wings.

Tiny monsters

If insects were as big as humans they would look like monsters!

What lives in my backyard — with 8 legs or more?

1 2 3 4 5 6 7 8

Spiders

Spiders have eight legs — count them!

Spider's web

Spiders build webs like this to trap insects. When an insect gets caught in the web, the spider goes to lunch!

Redback spiders

Take care — redback spiders bite! Can you see why they are called "redback" spiders?

Funnel-web spiders

Some spider bites can make you very, very sick. If you see a funnel-web, don't touch it!

Scorpions

Scorpions hide under logs and rocks. A scorpion has a nasty sting on the tip of its tail.

Ticks

Blood-sucking insects like this tick climb up plants and wait for people to brush against them.

Centipedes

Centipedes hunt other small creatures. They have powerful jaws, which they use to bite their prey.

Can you find the animals hidden in my backyard?

Some of the animals that you have seen on the previous pages are hiding in this backyard.

Can you find them?

All the animals have names beginning with...

B

Backyard begins with "B".

Butterfly
Beetle
Bee
Bandicoot
Blue-tongue lizard
Bat
Brushtail possum

What can you find down by the old fence?

An old wooden fence surrounds my backyard. On the fence and close by, I can often see lots of creatures. You've met some of these creatures before and know what they are. See if you can find them in this picture.

Butterflies	Bearded dragon	Wasp
Grasshopper	Redback spider	Ticks
Termites	Ants	Bee

What can you find down around the back of the house?

Find the animals with these shapes around the back of the house.

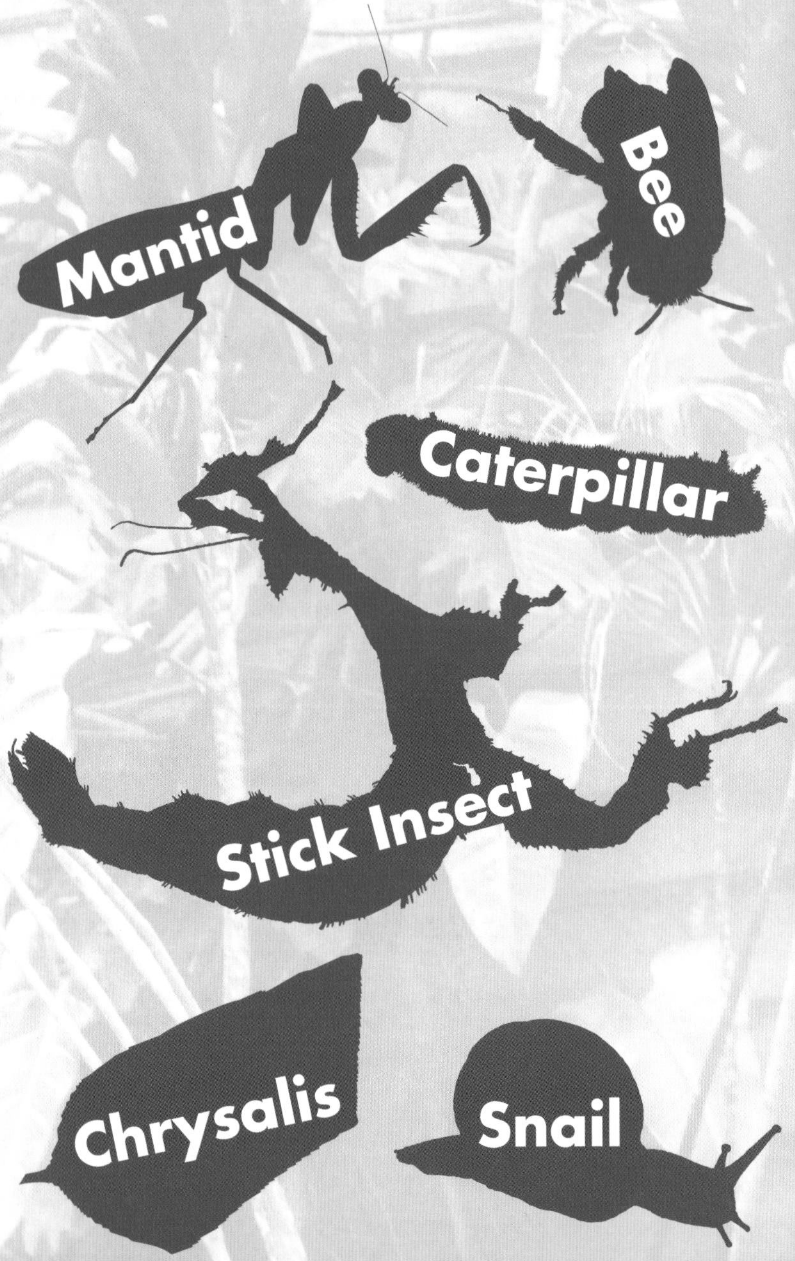

Mantid
Bee
Caterpillar
Stick Insect
Chrysalis
Snail

What eats what in my backyard?

Follow the arrows from the animals on this page to see what other animals eat it!

Wasps

Paper wasps build nests under eaves. They sting when you get too close to their nests. So watch out!

Flies & bugs

Flying insects are often caught in the air by birds that visit or live in my backyard.

Mice

Mice hide in small spaces, even behind the walls where they can't be seen — but some animals can find them!

Spiders

After spinning a web a spider waits for food to fly past and get caught in its sticky trap!

Swallows

Swallows catch their food in flight. They are very good fliers.

Snakes

Wherever mice hide, snakes can find them. Snakes can squeeze into very small spaces.

Owls

During the daytime, owls sleep in old barns and sheds. At night they go hunting for mice.

25

What are these animals doing on my lawn?

On a bare patch of lawn...

Watch out! Plovers swoop and dive at anyone who comes near their eggs.

Plovers sometimes lay their eggs on a bare patch of ground or lawn ... even in your backyard.

Plovers find seeds, worms, grubs and insects in the grass.

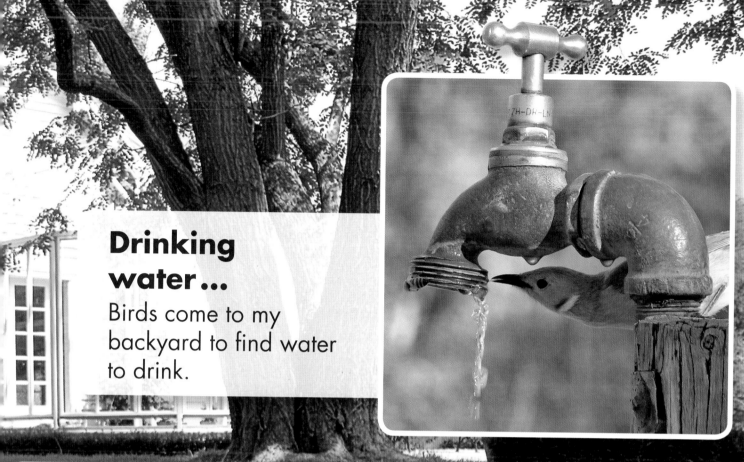

Drinking water...

Birds come to my backyard to find water to drink.

Eating grass...

Wombats, wallabies and many other animals like my backyard because it's covered in green grass — good enough to eat!

What animals do I find when I dig?

Animals underground

I like to dig holes and plant things in my backyard. Sometimes I find tiny animals in the soil.

Termites

These little creatures live in the soil and munch away on anything made of wood. They even eat tree trunks, fence posts and houses!

Mole crickets

Claws that work like shovels help the mole cricket burrow into the soil. From its underground home, it "sings" through the night, calling to its friends.

Cockroaches

Lift up a rotten log or a pile of leaves and you will probably find a cockroach or two. Cockroaches don't like to be out in the open and quickly scurry for cover.

Larvae

Many grubs in the soil are the larvae of insects. Some insects lay their eggs in the soil and grubs (larvae) hatch from the eggs. Later the grubs change their shape and become adult insects.

Earthworms

Earthworms don't have any eyes. They don't need them because they live underground where it is always dark!

Why are old trees so important for our wildlife?

Frogs are at home in the trees. Here they catch and eat insects that like to feed on flowers and leaves.

Green tree snakes hide among the branches, searching for frogs and lizards to eat.

Gliders and possums set up homes in the old hollows of tree trunks.

Insects fly, creep, crawl and burrow through trees, looking to eat flowers, nectar, pollen, leaves, bark or roots.

Birds build their nests among the branches or in any tree hollows that are large enough for them to squeeze into.

Flowers make pollen and nectar, which are food for animals that visit the trees in my backyard.

What do bird songs really mean?

Bird calls

Every morning the birds in my backyard sing to the birds in my neighbour's backyard. Here is what they say ...

Some birds twitter

Birds twitter and chirp noisily as they move about the yard. They tell their friends what's good to eat.

Some birds laugh

When Kookaburras "laugh" they are telling the kookaburras next door to stay out of their backyard.

Some birds sing, "come and play!"

Sometimes the boy birds in my yard invite the girl birds in my neighbour's yard to come over and play.

Some birds warble

Every morning the magpies sing loudly in my backyard. Magpies sing to tell the birds in the next street that they are awake.

What do animals do in the day and night?

Most birds fly during the day using their keen eyes to see.

Nesting

Some animals use the daylight to find materials to build their nests or line their hollows.

Soaring

When eagles, hawks and kites fly over my backyard, the other birds head for cover.

When the sun goes down the animals of the night come out to hunt and play.

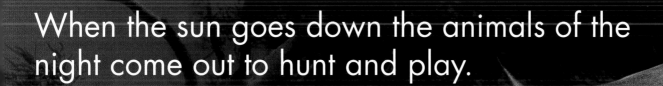

Finding
Bats come out at night when other animals cannot see them. Some bats catch insects to eat.

Gliding
Squirrel and sugar gliders can't fly but they can glide a long way. It's much safer to glide at night than during the day.

Hunting
Owls hunt at night. They use their sharp hearing and eyesight to find their food.

The animals in my backyard hop, crawl and run

Grasshoppers hop
Trace the grasshopper's tracks as it hops from place to place.

Bugs scurry
This bug is in a hurry. Chase it with your finger.

Follow their tracks with your finger

Snails slither
Slide your finger along the snail's trail. Make a slippery loop.

Lizards crawl
Lizards go round and round the fence post in my backyard.

Who is hiding in my backyard?

Waiting and watching

It's best to watch without being seen. This kestrel waits patiently for something to stir.

Staying very still

By looking like a twig, the stick insect hides itself from its enemies.

Matching the surrounds

The green feathers of the king-parrot are the same colour as leaves.

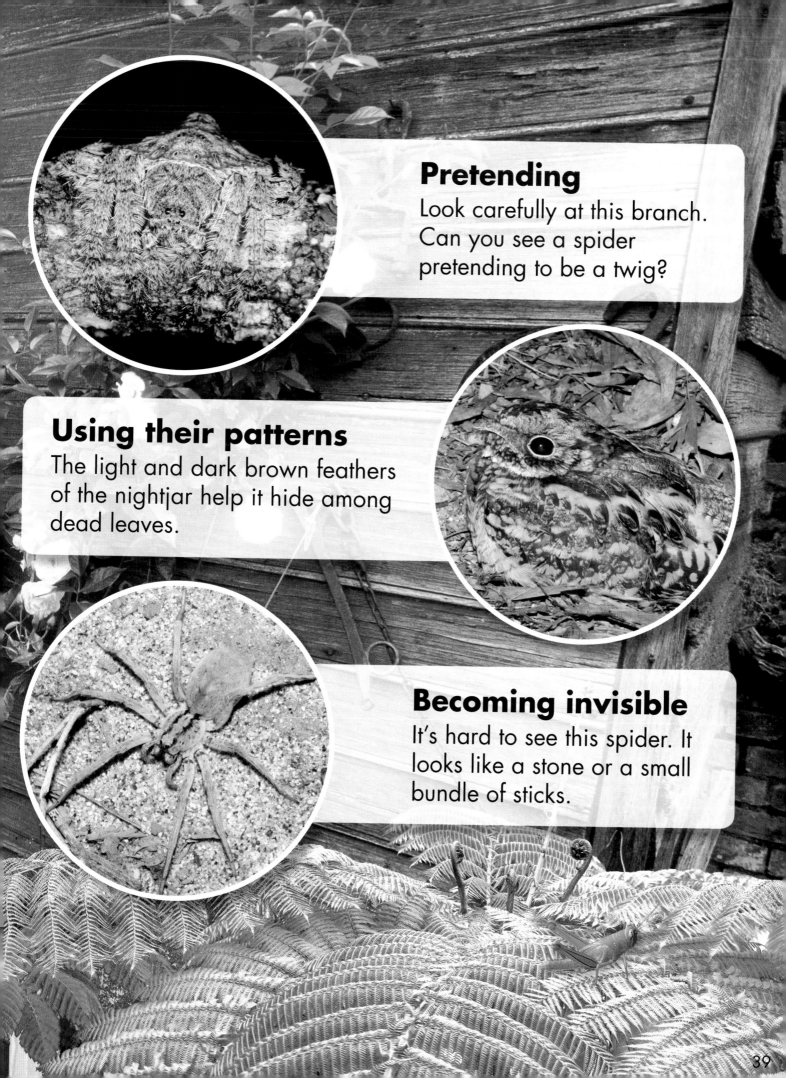

Pretending

Look carefully at this branch. Can you see a spider pretending to be a twig?

Using their patterns

The light and dark brown feathers of the nightjar help it hide among dead leaves.

Becoming invisible

It's hard to see this spider. It looks like a stone or a small bundle of sticks.

Should I feed the animals in my backyard?

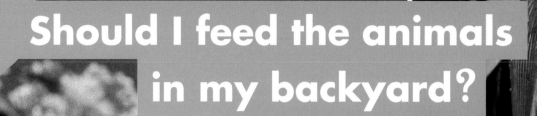

What food is best for native animals to eat?

Animals such as the brushtail possum like to eat many different kinds of food. Some food is good for them. Some food is not. Eating too much of the wrong food can make animals sick. Human food is good for people but it is not always good for animals. Animals sometimes have to eat fruit and vegetables too!

Possum food

Possums eat many different plants that grow in the bush and in our backyard garden.

Unhealthy food

When animals eat from the same plates as we do, we share our food and they share their diseases. Don't leave any food lying around!

People food

People can sometimes be messy eaters. Many animals love to eat our table scraps. So make sure you clean up your mess!

Who's making all that noise at night?

There are lots of animals that make noises at night. They sound scary in the dark but they are very cute.

Listen for them when you lie in bed. They might even sing you to sleep.

"Snore, snore!"
When my sister snores she frightens all the animals away!

Possums

"*Scratch, scratch!*" Possums are running around in your ceiling.

Geckoes

"*Yip! Yip!*" Geckoes bark at one another in the dark.

Frogmouths

"*Hooom, hooom!*" A frogmouth's call keeps echoing during the night.

Fruit bats

"*Squabble, squabble!*" Sometimes you can hear fruit bats eating fruit in the trees.

Frogs

"*Croak, croak!*" Frogs can even croak louder than my sister's snoring!

Shhhhhhh ...
The animals are resting!

Mum and dad

When many of the animals are asleep, my mum and dad are hard at work. There are so many things to do to do ...

Flowers to be watered ...
Weeds to be pulled ...
Gate to be fixed ...
Gutters to be cleared ...
Windows to be washed ...

Branches to be trimmed ...
Fence to be painted ...
Holes to be dug ...
Leaves to be raked ...
Lawns to be mowed ...

... I hope they don't wake up the animals who sleep in our backyard.

Is there room for my pets?

Rover is my pet dog.
Rover loves to bark and chase things.

So, I have to make sure Rover doesn't chase away the other animals. I put a leash on him, take him for long walks and give him plenty of exercise. I never let him chase koalas or possums or any of the other animals that share my backyard.

Sylvester is my pet cat.

I look after him and make sure he is well-fed.

I put a bell around his neck and I keep him indoors at night so he doesn't hunt and kill the other animals in my yard.

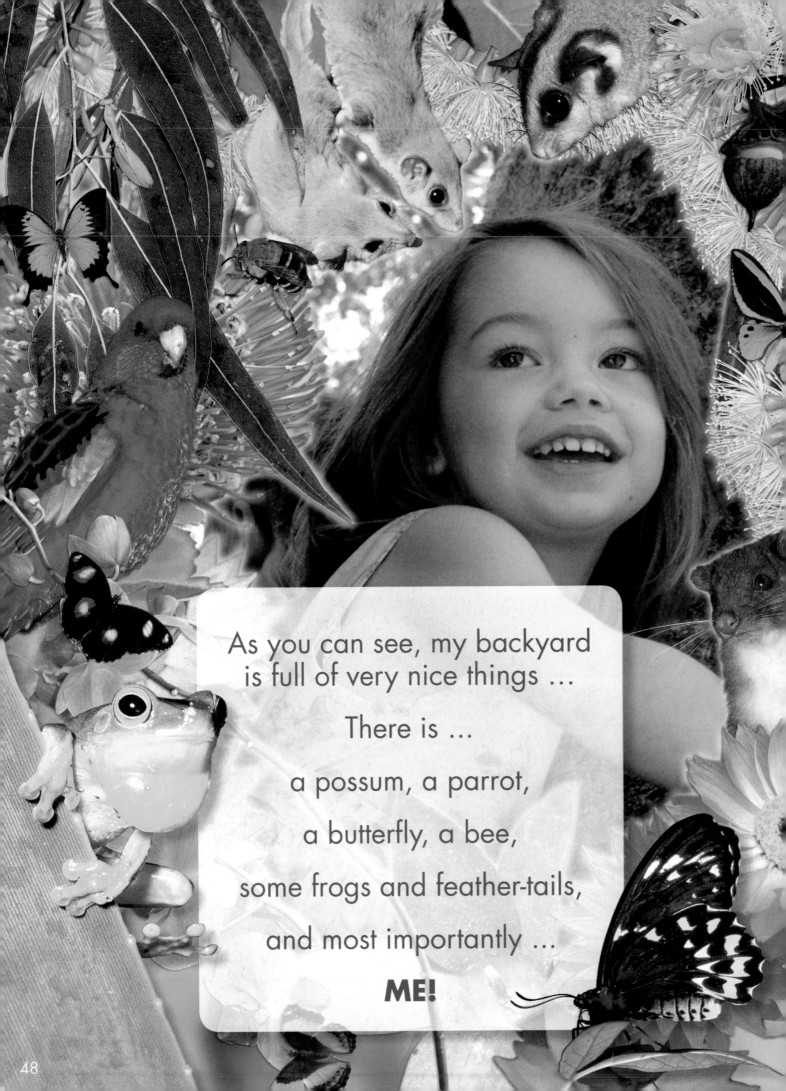

As you can see, my backyard is full of very nice things ...

There is ...

a possum, a parrot,

a butterfly, a bee,

some frogs and feather-tails,

and most importantly ...

ME!